This book belongs to

Pre-Primer	Primer	First	Second	Third
a	all	after	always	about
and	am	again	around	better
away	are	an	because	bring
big	at	any	been	carry
blue	ate	as	before	clean
can	be	ask	best	cut
come	black	by	both	done
down	brown	could	buy	draw
find	but	every	call	drink
for	came	fly	cold	eight
funny	did	from	does	fall
go	do	give	don't	far
help	eat	going	fast	full
here	four	had	first	got
I	get	has	five	grow
in	good	her	found	hold
is	have	him	gave	hot
it	he	his	goes	hurt
jump	into	how	green	if
little	like	just	its	keep
look	must	know	made	kind
make	new	let	many	laugh
me	no	live	off	light
my	now	may	or	long
not	on	of	pull	much
one	our	old	red	myself
play	out	once	right	never
red	please	open	sing	only
run	pretty	over	sit	own
said	ran	put	sleep	pick
see	ride	round	tell	seven
the	saw	some	their	shall
three	say	stop	these	show
to	she	take	those	six
two	so	thank	upon	small
up	soon	then	us	start
we	that	them	use	ten
where	there	think	very	today
yellow	they	walk	wash	together
you	this	were	which	try
	too	when	why	warm
	under		wish	
	want		work	
	was		would	
	well		write	
	went		your	
	what			
	white			
	who			
	will			
	with			
	yes			

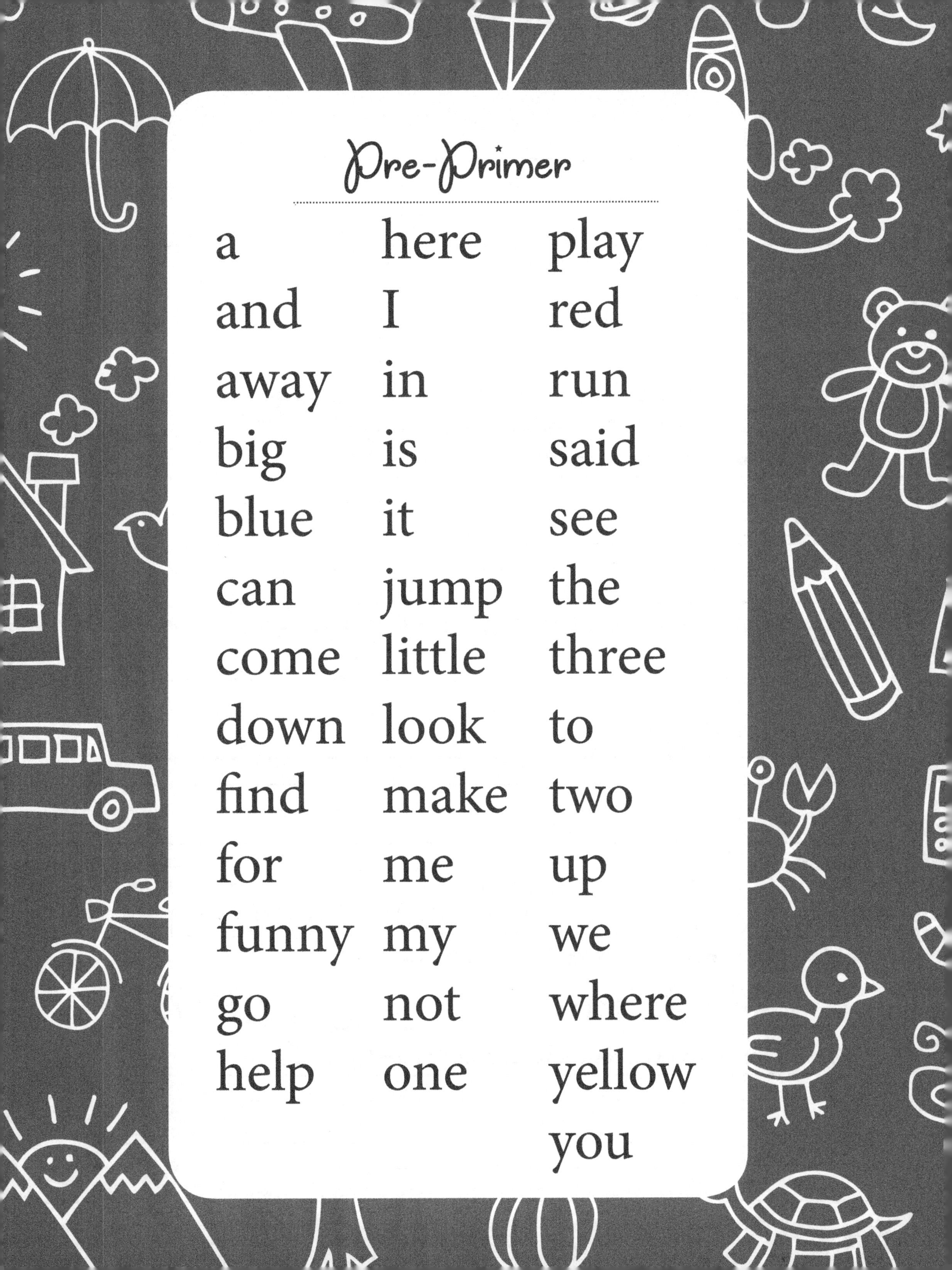

Pre-Primer

a
and
away
big
blue
can
come
down
find
for
funny
go
help

here
I
in
is
it
jump
little
look
make
me
my
not
one

play
red
run
said
see
the
three
to
two
up
we
where
yellow
you

Track.

Write.

Color.

a a a a a

Write the word to finish the sentence.

It is _________ cat.

Write your own sentence using the word <u>a</u>.

Track.

and and and

Write.

Color.

and and and

Write the word to finish the sentence.

My friend _________ I play.

Write your own sentence using the word <u>and</u>.

Track.

away away away

Write.

Color.

away away away

Write the word to finish the sentence.

The bird flew __________ .

Write your own sentence using the word <u>away.</u>

Track.

big big big

Write.

Color.

big big big

Write the word to finish the sentence.

My ball is __________ .

Write your own sentence using the word <u>big.</u>

Track.

blue blue blue

Write.

Color.

blue blue blue

Write the word to finish the sentence.

The sky is __________ .

Write your own sentence using the word <u>blue.</u>

Track.

can can can

Write.

Color.

can can can

Write the word to finish the sentence.

I __________ brush my teeth.

Write your own sentence using the word <u>can.</u>

Track.

come come come

Write.

Color.

come come come

Write the word to finish the sentence.

Will you _______over?

Write your own sentence using the word **come.**

Track.

down down down

Write.

Color.

down down down

Write the word to finish the sentence.

We go up and _______ .

Write your own sentence using the word **down.**

Track.

find find find

Write.

Color.

find find find

Write the word to finish the sentence.

I can't _________ my pencil.

Write your own sentence using the word <u>find.</u>

Track.

for for for

Write.

Color.

for for for

Write the word to finish the sentence.

This is a gift _________ you.

Write your own sentence using the word <u>for.</u>

Track.

funny funny funny

Write.

Color.

funny funny

Write the word to finish the sentence.

Big brother is _______.

Write your own sentence using the word <u>funny.</u>

Track.

go   go   go

Write.

Color.

go   go   go   go

Write the word to finish the sentence.

The bus can _______.

Write your own sentence using the word <u>go.</u>

Track.

help help help

Write.

Color.

help help help

Write the word to finish the sentence.

I will _____________ you.

Write your own sentence using the word <u>help.</u>

Track.

here here here here

Write.

Color.

here here

Write the word to finish the sentence.

I am _______.

Write your own sentence using the word <u>here.</u>

Track.

Write.

Color.

Write the word to finish the sentence.

__________ see a kite up in the sky.

Write your own sentence using the word I.

Track.

in   in   in   in

Write.

Color.

in   in   in   in   in

Write the word to finish the sentence.

The rabbit is __________ the hole.

Write your own sentence using the word in.

Track.

is   is   is   is

Write.

Color.

is   is   is   is

Write the word to finish the sentence.

It_____________ not my hat.

Write your own sentence using the word <u>is.</u>

Track.

it   it   it   it

Write.

Color.

it   it   it   it

Write the word to finish the sentence.

We like _______.

Write your own sentence using the word <u>it.</u>

Track.

jump jump jump

Write.

Color.

jump jump jump

Write the word to finish the sentence.

I will _______ over the puddle.

Write your own sentence using the word <u>jump</u>.

Track.

little little little

Write.

Color.

little little little

Write the word to finish the sentence.

It was too _______ for me.

Write your own sentence using the word <u>little</u>.

Track.

look look look

Write.

Color.

look look look

Write the word to finish the sentence.

I will __________ in my desk.

Write your own sentence using the word __look.__

Track.

make make make

Write.

Color.

make make make

Write the word to finish the sentence.

I _______ my homework .

Write your own sentence using the word __make.__

Track.

me   me   me

Write.

Color.

me me me me

Write the word to finish the sentence.

My mom and dad love __________ .

Write your own sentence using the word <u>me.</u>

Track.

my   my   my

Write.

Color.

my my my my

Write the word to finish the sentence.

It is for __________ mom.

Write your own sentence using the word <u>my.</u>

Track.

not not not

Write.

Color.

not not not

Write the word to finish the sentence.

It is __________ my can.

Write your own sentence using the word <u>not.</u>

Track.

one one one

Write.

Color.

one one one

Write the word to finish the sentence.

Say which __________ you want.

Write your own sentence using the word <u>one.</u>

Track.

play play play

Write.

Color.

play play play

Write the word to finish the sentence.

Will you __________ tag with me?

Write your own sentence using the word play.

Track.

red red red

Write.

Color.

red red red red

Write the word to finish the sentence.

The apple is __________ .

Write your own sentence using the word red.

Track.

run run run

Write.

Color.

run run run

Write the word to finish the sentence.

I can __________ fast.

Write your own sentence using the word <u>run.</u>

Track.

said said said

Write.

Color.

said said said

Write the word to finish the sentence.

He __________ I was funny.

Write your own sentence using the word <u>said.</u>

Track.

see   see   see

Write.

Color.

see   see   see

Write the word to finish the sentence.

I can _______ the star.

Write your own sentence using the word <u>see.</u>

Track.

the   the   the

Write.

Color.

the   the   the

Write the word to finish the sentence.

She read _______ book.

Write your own sentence using the word <u>the.</u>

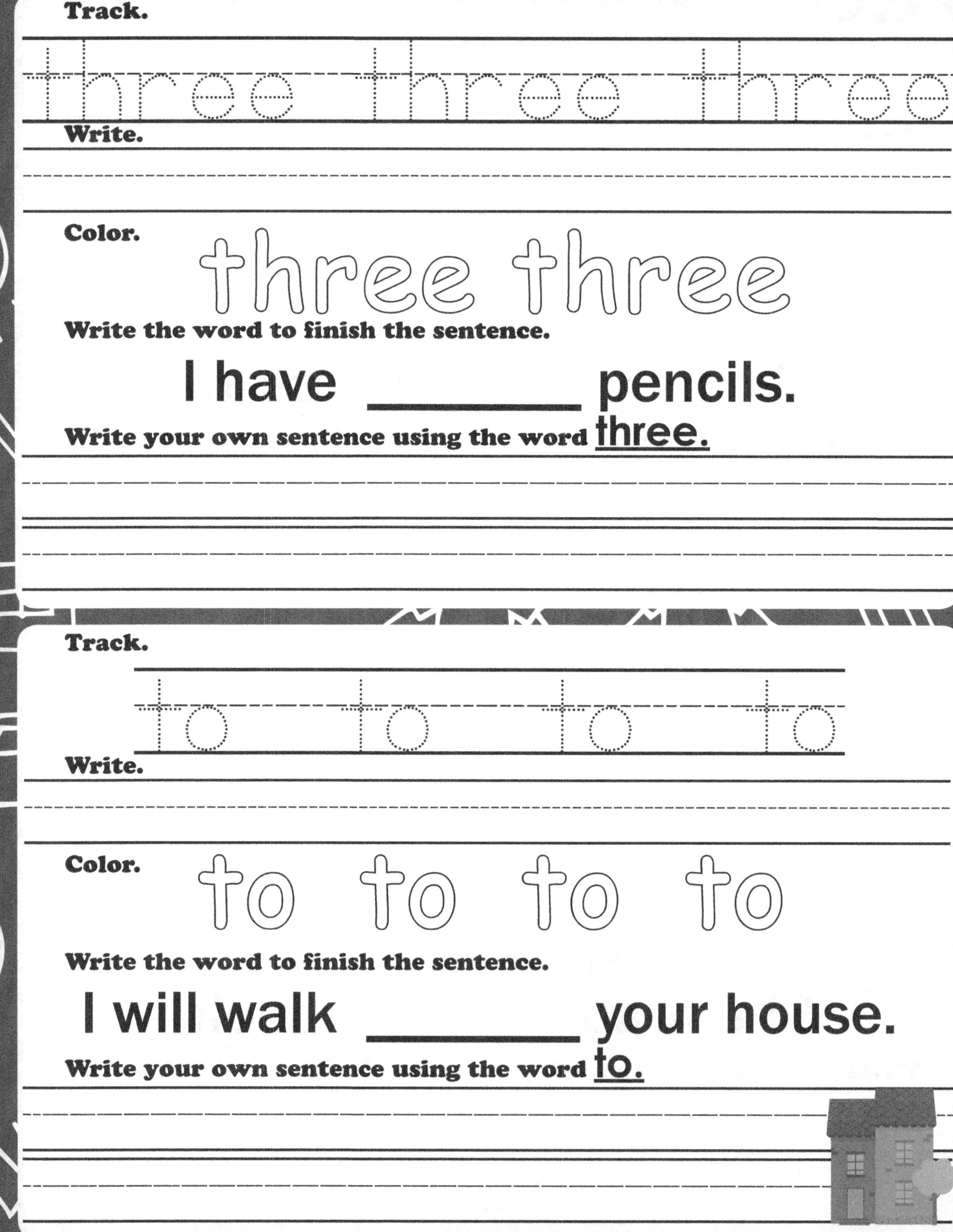

Track.

three three three

Write.

Color.

three three

Write the word to finish the sentence.

I have __________ pencils.

Write your own sentence using the word <u>three.</u>

Track.

to to to to

Write.

Color.

to to to to

Write the word to finish the sentence.

I will walk __________ your house.

Write your own sentence using the word <u>to.</u>

Track.

two two two

Write.

Color.

two two two

Write the word to finish the sentence.

There are _________ kids on the bus.

Write your own sentence using the word two.

Track.

up up up up

Write.

Color.

up up up up up

Write the word to finish the sentence.

The plane will go _________ .

Write your own sentence using the word up.

Track.

we   we   we   we

Write.

Color.

we we we we

Write the word to finish the sentence.

__________ are in first grade.

Write your own sentence using the word <u>we.</u>

Track.

where   where

Write.

Color.

where where

Write the word to finish the sentence.

__________ are you going?

Write your own sentence using the word <u>where.</u>

Track.

yellow yellow

Write.

Color.

yellow yellow

Write the word to finish the sentence.

The duck is __________.

Write your own sentence using the word <u>yellow</u>.

Track.

you   you   you

Write.

Color.

you   you   you

Write the word to finish the sentence.

__________ are beautiful.

Write your own sentence using the word <u>you</u>.

Primer

all	four	out	this
am	get	please	too
are	good	pretty	under
at	have	ran	want
ate	he	ride	was
be	into	saw	well
black	like	say	went
brown	must	she	what
but	new	so	white
came	no	soon	who
did	now	that	will
do	on	there	with
eat	our	they	yes

Track.

all all all all

Write.

Color.

all all all all all

Write the word to finish the sentence.

I ate _______ my lunch.

Write your own sentence using the word all.

Track.

am am am

Write.

Color.

am am am am

Write the word to finish the sentence.

I _______ a student.

Write your own sentence using the word am.

Track.

are are are

Write.

Color.

are are are

Write the word to finish the sentence.

We _______ happy.

Write your own sentence using the word <u>are</u>.

Track.

at at at at

Write.

Color.

at at at at

Write the word to finish the sentence.

I looked _______ the dog.

Write your own sentence using the word <u>at.</u>

Track.

ate ate ate

Write.

Color.

ate ate ate

Write the word to finish the sentence.

He ________ his snack.

Write your own sentence using the word <u>ate.</u>

Track.

be be be be

Write.

Color.

be be be be

Write the word to finish the sentence.

I will ________ kind.

Write your own sentence using the word <u>be.</u>

Track.

black black black

Write.

Color.

black black

Write the word to finish the sentence.

The car is _______.

Write your own sentence using the word <u>black.</u>

Track.

brown   brown

Write.

Color.

brown brown

Write the word to finish the sentence.

I saw a _______ bear.

Write your own sentence using the word <u>brown.</u>

Track.

but but but

Write.

Color.

but but but

Write the word to finish the sentence.

I took a nap,__________ I am still tired.

Write your own sentence using the word <u>but.</u>

Track.

came came came

Write.

Color.

came came came

Write the word to finish the sentence.

My cousins __________ for a visit.

Write your own sentence using the word <u>came.</u>

Track.

Write.

Color.

did did did did

Write the word to finish the sentence.

She _______ her homework.

Write your own sentence using the word <u>did.</u>

Track.

Write.

Color.

do do do do

Write the word to finish the sentence.

_______ you like flower?

Write your own sentence using the word <u>do.</u>

Track.

eat eat eat

Write.

Color.

eat eat eat

Write the word to finish the sentence.

I _______ breakfast.

Write your own sentence using the word <u>eat</u>.

Track.

four four four

Write.

Color.

four four four

Write the word to finish the sentence.

There are _______ of us.

Write your own sentence using the word <u>four</u>.

Track.

get   get   get

Write.

Color.

get get get

Write the word to finish the sentence.

They will _______ a gold slip.

Write your own sentence using the word <u>get</u>.

Track.

good   good   good

Write.

Color.

good good good

Write the word to finish the sentence.

You did a _______ job!

Write your own sentence using the word <u>good</u>.

Track.

have   have   have

Write.

Color.

have have have

Write the word to finish the sentence.

I _______ many white hats.

Write your own sentence using the word <u>have.</u>

Track.

he   he   he   he

Write.

Color.

he he he he

Write the word to finish the sentence.

_______ is my brother.

Write your own sentence using the word <u>he.</u>

Track.

into into into

Write.

Color.

into into into

Write the word to finish the sentence.

I walked _________ the store.

Write your own sentence using the word <u>into.</u>

Track.

like like like

Write.

Color.

like like like

Write the word to finish the sentence.

I _________ ice - cream.

Write your own sentence using the word <u>like.</u>

Track.

must must must

Write.

Color.

must must must

Write the word to finish the sentence.

I _______ go now.

Write your own sentence using the word <u>must.</u>

Track.

new new new

Write.

Color.

new new new

Write the word to finish the sentence.

It is _______ shirt.

Write your own sentence using the word <u>new.</u>

Track.

no   no   no   no

Write.

Color.

no no no no no

Write the word to finish the sentence.

My mom says the answer is _______.

Write your own sentence using the word <u>no</u>.

Track.

now   now   now

Write.

Color.

now now now

Write the word to finish the sentence.

We have Music _______.

Write your own sentence using the word <u>now</u>.

Track.

on   on   on   on

Write.

Color.

on on on on on

Write the word to finish the sentence.

She sat _______ the swing.

Write your own sentence using the word <u>on.</u>

Track.

our   our   our

Write.

Color.

our our our

Write the word to finish the sentence.

They like _______ cat.

Write your own sentence using the word <u>our.</u>

Track.

out out out

Write.

Color.

out out out

Write the word to finish the sentence.

All four boys went _______ the door.

Write your own sentence using the word <u>out</u>.

Track.

please please

Write.

Color.

please please

Write the word to finish the sentence.

Can I _______ go to the party?

Write your own sentence using the word <u>please</u>.

Track.

pretty pretty

Write.

Color.

pretty pretty

Write the word to finish the sentence.

She is _______ girl.

Write your own sentence using the word pretty.

Track.

ran ran ran

Write.

Color.

ran ran ran

Write the word to finish the sentence.

My cat _______ away.

Write your own sentence using the word ran.

Track.

ride   ride   ride

Write.

Color.

ride ride ride

Write the word to finish the sentence.

I went on a roller coaster __________ .

Write your own sentence using the word ride.

Track.

saw   saw   saw

Write.

Color.

saw   saw   saw

Write the word to finish the sentence.

He __________ a ghost.

Write your own sentence using the word saw.

Track.

say say say

Write.

Color.

say say say

Write the word to finish the sentence.

What did you __________?

Write your own sentence using the word <u>say</u>.

Track.

she she she

Write.

Color.

she she she

Write the word to finish the sentence.

__________ is my mother

Write your own sentence using the word <u>she</u>.

Track.

SO   SO   SO   SO

Write.

Color.

SO SO SO SO SO

Write the word to finish the sentence.

I am _______ hungry.

Write your own sentence using the word <u>SO.</u>

Track.

soon   soon   soon

Write.

Color.

soon soon soon

Write the word to finish the sentence.

I will be done _______ .

Write your own sentence using the word <u>soon.</u>

Track.

that that that

Write.

Color.

that that that

Write the word to finish the sentence.

I saw _________ show on TV.

Write your own sentence using the word <u>that.</u>

Track.

there there there

Write.

Color.

there there

Write the word to finish the sentence.

Put it over _________.

Write your own sentence using the word <u>there.</u>

Track.

they they they

Write.

Color.

they they they

Write the word to finish the sentence.

_______ always walk in the hall.

Write your own sentence using the word <u>they</u>.

Track.

this this this

Write.

Color.

this this this

Write the word to finish the sentence.

_______ is my friend.

Write your own sentence using the word <u>this</u>.

Track.

too too too

Write.

Color.

too too too too

Write the word to finish the sentence.

I have _______ many books.

Write your own sentence using the word <u>too</u>.

Track.

under under

Write.

Color.

under under

Write the word to finish the sentence.

There is a monster _______ my bed.

Write your own sentence using the word <u>under</u>.

Track.

want want want

Write.

Color.

want want want

Write the word to finish the sentence.

I _______ a cookie.

Write your own sentence using the word <u>want.</u>

Track.

was was was

Write.

Color.

was was was

Write the word to finish the sentence.

He _______ running down the hall.

Write your own sentence using the word <u>was.</u>

Track.

well well well

Write.

Color.

well well well

Write the word to finish the sentence.

I don't feel __________ .

Write your own sentence using the word <u>well</u>.

Track.

went went went

Write.

Color.

went went

Write the word to finish the sentence.

We __________ to the movies.

Write your own sentence using the word <u>went</u>.

Track.

what what what

Write.

Color.

what what what

Write the word to finish the sentence.

__________ is your name?

Write your own sentence using the word what.

Track.

white white

Write.

Color.

white white

Write the word to finish the sentence.

to the movies __________ .

Write your own sentence using the word white.

Track.

who   who   who

Write.

Color.

who who who

Write the word to finish the sentence.

_______ is there with you?

Write your own sentence using the word <u>who.</u>

Track.

will   will   will

Write.

Color.

will will will

Write the word to finish the sentence.

I _______ go to supermarket.

Write your own sentence using the word <u>will.</u>

Track.

with   with   with

Write.

Color.

with with with

Write the word to finish the sentence.

I play__________ you.

Write your own sentence using the word <u>with.</u>

Track.

yes   yes   yes

Write.

Color.

yes yes yes

Write the word to finish the sentence.

__________, I like using the computer .

Write your own sentence using the word <u>yes.</u>

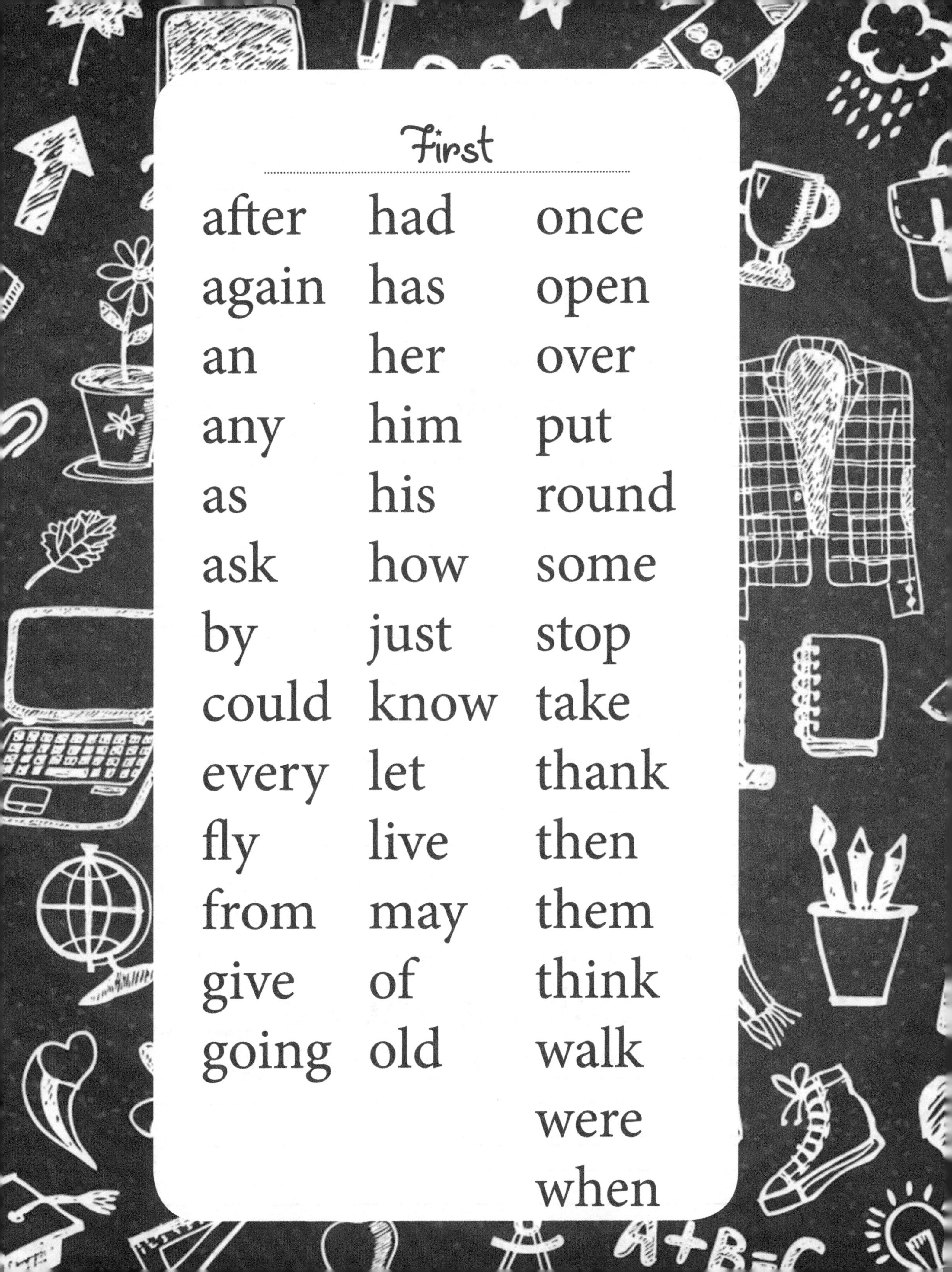

First

after
again
an
any
as
ask
by
could
every
fly
from
give
going

had
has
her
him
his
how
just
know
let
live
may
of
old

once
open
over
put
round
some
stop
take
thank
then
them
think
walk
were
when

Track.

after after after

Write.

Color.

after after

Write the word to finish the sentence.

Read your book _________ school.

Write your own sentence using the word <u>after</u>.

Track.

again again again

Write.

Color.

again again again

Write the word to finish the sentence.

Did you watch the movie _________ ?

Write your own sentence using the word <u>again</u>.

Track.

an   an   an   an

Write.

Color.

an an an an an

Write the word to finish the sentence.

I saw _______ elephant at the zoo.

Write your own sentence using the word **an.**

Track.

any   any   any

Write.

Color.

any any any

Write the word to finish the sentence.

I didn't see _______ whales.

Write your own sentence using the word **any.**

Track.

as   as   as   as

Write.

Color.

as   as   as   as   as

Write the word to finish the sentence.

I am _________ quiet as a mouse.

Write your own sentence using the word <u>as.</u>

Track.

ask   ask   ask

Write.

Color.

ask   ask   ask

Write the word to finish the sentence.

Did you _________ the teacher?

Write your own sentence using the word <u>ask.</u>

Track.

by by by by

Write.

Color.

by by by by

Write the word to finish the sentence.

Sit __________ your friend.

Write your own sentence using the word <u>by</u>.

Track.

could could could

Write.

Color.

could could

Write the word to finish the sentence.

__________ you get some for her?

Write your own sentence using the word <u>could</u>.

Track.

every every

Write.

Color.

every every

Write the word to finish the sentence.

I like _______ book on the shelf.

Write your own sentence using the word **every.**

Track.

fly fly fly fly

Write.

Color. fly fly fly fly

Write the word to finish the sentence.

The bird wil _______ to the nest.

Write your own sentence using the word **ask.**

Track.

from from from

Write.

Color.

from from from

Write the word to finish the sentence.

I got a dime __________ my mom.

Write your own sentence using the word <u>from.</u>

Track.

give give give

Write.

Color.

give give give

Write the word to finish the sentence.

__________ Tommy his paper.

Write your own sentence using the word <u>give.</u>

Track.

going going going

Write.

Color.

going going going

Write the word to finish the sentence.

I am _________ to see a movie.

Write your own sentence using the word going.

Track.

had had had

Write.

Color.

had had had

Write the word to finish the sentence.

I _________ a great time.

Write your own sentence using the word had.

Track.

has has has

Write.

Color.

has has has

Write the word to finish the sentence.

He _______ a folder on her desk.

Write your own sentence using the word <u>has.</u>

Track.

her her her

Write.

Color.

her her her

Write the word to finish the sentence.

That belongs to _______.

Write your own sentence using the word <u>her.</u>

Track.
Write.
Color.
him him him
Write the word to finish the sentence.
I watched _______ play baseball.
Write your own sentence using the word him.
Track.
Write.
Color.
his his his
Write the word to finish the sentence.
He hung _______ coat on a hook.
Write your own sentence using the word his.

Track.

how how how

Write.

Color.

how how how

Write the word to finish the sentence.

__________ did you do that?

Write your own sentence using the word <u>how.</u>

Track.

just just just

Write.

Color.

just just just

Write the word to finish the sentence.

He came in __________ now.

Write your own sentence using the word <u>just.</u>

Track.

know know know

Write.

Color.

know know know

Write the word to finish the sentence.

I ________ how to sing.

Write your own sentence using the word <u>know.</u>

Track.

let let let let

Write.

Color.

let let let let

Write the word to finish the sentence.

Please________ her use your crayon.

Write your own sentence using the word <u>let.</u>

Track.

live   live   live

Write.

Color.

live live live

Write the word to finish the sentence.

I _______ in Cresco.

Write your own sentence using the word <u>live.</u>

Track.

may   may   may

Write.

Color.

may may may

Write the word to finish the sentence.

You _______ go play.

Write your own sentence using the word <u>may.</u>

Track.

of   of   of   of

Write.

Color.

of of of of of

Write the word to finish the sentence.

I had a lot _______ fun.

Write your own sentence using the word <u>of</u>.

Track.

old   old   old

Write.

Color.

old   old   old

Write the word to finish the sentence.

My sneakers are _______ .

Write your own sentence using the word <u>old</u>.

Track.

once once once

Write.

Color.

once once once

Write the word to finish the sentence.

Stop talking at ________!

Write your own sentence using the word <u>once</u>.

Track.

open open open

Write.

Color.

open open open

Write the word to finish the sentence.

Leave the door ________ .

Write your own sentence using the word <u>open</u>.

Track.

over over over

Write.

Color.

over over over

Write the word to finish the sentence.

Can you come _______ to my house?

Write your own sentence using the word <u>over</u>.

Track.

put put put

Write.

Color.

put put put

Write the word to finish the sentence.

I will _______ the book on the shelf.

Write your own sentence using the word <u>put</u>.

Track.

Write.

Color.

Write the word to finish the sentence.

The ball is _______ .

Write your own sentence using the word <u>round.</u>

Track.

Write.

Color.

Write the word to finish the sentence.

Can I have _______ ?

Write your own sentence using the word <u>some.</u>

Track.

stop   stop   stop

Write.

Color.

stop stop stop

Write the word to finish the sentence.

It is time to _________ .

Write your own sentence using the word <u>stop.</u>

Track.

take   take   take

Write.

Color.

take take

Write the word to finish the sentence.

I will _________ my folder home.

Write your own sentence using the word <u>take.</u>

Track.

thank   thank

Write.

Color.

thank thank

Write the word to finish the sentence.

_______ you for helping me.

Write your own sentence using the word **thank.**

Track.

then   then   then

Write.

Color.

then then then

Write the word to finish the sentence.

I will eat lunch and_______ go play.

Write your own sentence using the word **then.**

Track.

them them them

Write.

Color.

them them them

Write the word to finish the sentence.

That ball belongs to _________ .

Write your own sentence using the word <u>them</u>.

think **Track.**

think think think

Write.

Color.

think think

Write the word to finish the sentence.

I _________ it is your turn.

Write your own sentence using the word <u>think</u>.

Track.

walk   walk   walk

Write.

Color.

walk walk walk

Write the word to finish the sentence.

Let's go for a __________ .

Write your own sentence using the word <u>walk.</u>

Track.

were   were   were

Write.

Color.

were were were

Write the word to finish the sentence.

They __________ having a good time.

Write your own sentence using the word <u>were.</u>

Track.

when when when

Write.

Color.

when when when

Write the word to finish the sentence.

_______ are we leaving?

Write your own sentence using the word <u>when.</u>

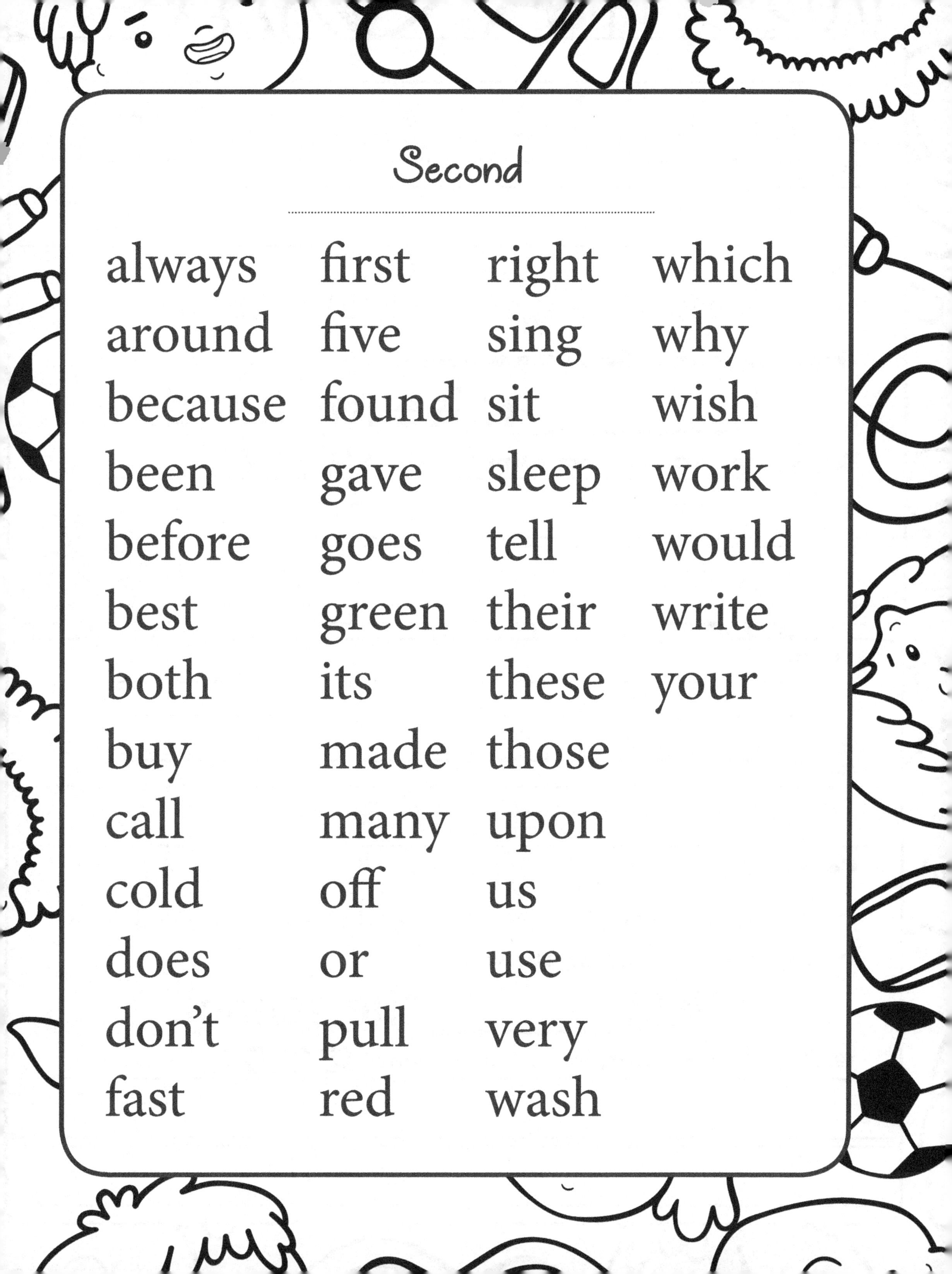

Second

always	first	right	which
around	five	sing	why
because	found	sit	wish
been	gave	sleep	work
before	goes	tell	would
best	green	their	write
both	its	these	your
buy	made	those	
call	many	upon	
cold	off	us	
does	or	use	
don't	pull	very	
fast	red	wash	

Track.

always always

Write.

Color.

always alway

Write the word to finish the sentence.

I _______ raise my hand.

Write your own sentence using the word <u>alway</u>.

Track.

around around

Write.

Color.

around around

Write the word to finish the sentence.

Walk _______ the school.

Write your own sentence using the word <u>around</u>.

Track.

because   because

Write.

Color.

because because

Write the word to finish the sentence.

I like school _______ it is fun.

Write your own sentence using the word because.

Track.

been   been   been

Write.

Color.

been been

Write the word to finish the sentence.

It has _______ raining for two days.

Write your own sentence using the word been.

Track.

before before

Write.

Color.

before before

Write the word to finish the sentence.

Wash your hands _______ you eat.

Write your own sentence using the word **before.**

Track.

best best best

Write.

Color.

best best

Write the word to finish the sentence.

That was the _______ time I ever had.

Write your own sentence using the word **best.**

Track.

both both both

Write.

Color.

both both both

Write the word to finish the sentence.

We _______ went for a walk.

Write your own sentence using the word both.

Track.

buy buy buy

Write.

Color.

buy buy buy

Write the word to finish the sentence.

I will _______ apple.

Write your own sentence using the word buy.

Track.

call   call   call

Write.

Color.

call call call

Write the word to finish the sentence.

Please _______ me back.

Write your own sentence using the word <u>call.</u>

Track.

cold   cold   cold

Write.

Color.

cold cold cold

Write the word to finish the sentence.

It is very _______ today.

Write your own sentence using the word <u>cold.</u>

Track.

does does does

Write.

Color.

does does does

Write the word to finish the sentence.

How much _______ he bring?

Write your own sentence using the word does.

Track.

don't don't

Write.

Color.

don't don't don't

Write the word to finish the sentence.

_______ cut in line.

Write your own sentence using the word don't.

Track.

fast   fast   fast

Write.

Color.

fast fast fast

Write the word to finish the sentence.

He is __________.

Write your own sentence using the word <u>fast.</u>

Track.

first   first   first

Write.

Color.

first first

Write the word to finish the sentence.

__________ grade is great!

Write your own sentence using the word <u>first.</u>

Track.

five five five

Write.

Color.

five five five

Write the word to finish the sentence.

A nickel is worth ________ cents.

Write your own sentence using the word <u>five</u>.

Track.

found found

Write.

Color.

found found

Write the word to finish the sentence.

I ________ my scissors in my desk.

Write your own sentence using the word <u>found</u>.

Track.

gave gave gave

Write.

Color.

gave gave gave

Write the word to finish the sentence.

My mom _______ me a snack.

Write your own sentence using the word <u>gave.</u>

Track.

goes goes goes

Write.

Color.

goes goes goes

Write the word to finish the sentence.

He _______ to kindergarten.

Write your own sentence using the word <u>goes.</u>

Track.

green green

Write.

Color.

green green

Write the word to finish the sentence.

The grass is _______ .

Write your own sentence using the word <u>green.</u>

Track.

its its its its

Write.

Color.

its its its its

Write the word to finish the sentence.

The skunk lifts_______ tail.

Write your own sentence using the word <u>its.</u>

Track.

made made made

Write.

Color.

made made made

Write the word to finish the sentence.

I _______ my bed.

Write your own sentence using the word <u>made.</u>

Track.

many many many

Write.

Color.

many many many

Write the word to finish the sentence.

How _______ pets do you have?

Write your own sentence using the word <u>many.</u>

Track.

off off off

Write.

Color.

off off off

Write the word to finish the sentence.

Turn _______ the light.

Write your own sentence using the word <u>off.</u>

Track.

or or or or

Write.

Color.

or or or or or

Write the word to finish the sentence.

Do you like chocolate _______ vanilla?

Write your own sentence using the word <u>or.</u>

Track.

pull pull pull

Write.

Color.

pull pull pull

Write the word to finish the sentence.

The horse will _______ the carriage.

Write your own sentence using the word <u>pull</u>.

Track.

red red red

Write.

Color.

red red red

Write the word to finish the sentence.

I would like an apple that is _______ .

Write your own sentence using the word <u>red</u>.

Track.

right right right

Write.

Color.

right right

Write the word to finish the sentence.

That is the _______ answer.

Write your own sentence using the word right.

Track.

sing sing sing

Write.

Color.

sing sing sing

Write the word to finish the sentence.

Let's _______ a song.

Write your own sentence using the word sing.

Track.

sit sit sit sit

Write.

Color.

sit sit sit sit

Write the word to finish the sentence.

Please _______ down.

Write your own sentence using the word <u>sit.</u>

Track.

sleep sleep sleep

Write.

Color.

sleep sleep

Write the word to finish the sentence.

The baby will _______ in the crib.

Write your own sentence using the word <u>sleep.</u>

Track.

tell   tell   tell   tell

Write.

Color.

tell tell tell

Write the word to finish the sentence.

Did you________ your dad?

Write your own sentence using the word <u>tell.</u>

Track.

their   their   their

Write.

Color.

their their

Write the word to finish the sentence.

The family got in ________ car.

Write your own sentence using the word <u>their.</u>

Track.

these these these

Write.

Color.

these these

Write the word to finish the sentence.

Do _______ books belong to you?

Write your own sentence using the word **these.**

Track.

those those those

Write.

Color.

those those

Write the word to finish the sentence.

Put _______ books on the desk.

Write your own sentence using the word **those.**

Track.

upon   upon   upon

Write.

Color.

upon   upon   upon

Write the word to finish the sentence.

One _______ a time there was a frog.

Write your own sentence using the word upon.

Track.

us   us   us   us

Write.

Color.

us us us us us

Write the word to finish the sentence.

Read _______ a story.

Write your own sentence using the word US.

Track.

use use use

Write.

Color.

use use use

Write the word to finish the sentence.

Please _______ an inside voice.

Write your own sentence using the word use.

Track.

very very very

Write.

Color.

very very very

Write the word to finish the sentence.

I am _______ tired.

Write your own sentence using the word very.

Track.

wash wash wash

Write.

Color.

wash wash wash

Write the word to finish the sentence.

I will _______ the dishes.

Write your own sentence using the word <u>wash.</u>

Track.

which which

Write.

Color.

which which

Write the word to finish the sentence.

_______ one is yours?

Write your own sentence using the word <u>which.</u>

Track.

why why why

Write.

Color.

why why why

Write the word to finish the sentence.

_______ did you leave?

Write your own sentence using the word <u>why.</u>

Track.

wish wish wish

Write.

Color.

wish wish wish

Write the word to finish the sentence.

I _______ it was time to go home.

Write your own sentence using the word <u>wish.</u>

Track.

work   work   work

Write.

Color.

work work work

Write the word to finish the sentence.

Finish your _______ .

Write your own sentence using the word <u>work.</u>

Track.

would   would   would

Write.

Color.

would would

Write the word to finish the sentence.

What _______ you like for dinner?

Write your own sentence using the word <u>would.</u>

Track.

write write write

Write.

Color.

write write write

Write the word to finish the sentence.

Did you _______ in your journal?

Write your own sentence using the word <u>write.</u>

Track.

your your your

Write.

Color.

your your your

Write the word to finish the sentence.

I saw _______ teacher in the hall.

Write your own sentence using the word <u>your.</u>

Third

about	got	never	try
better	grow	only	warm
bring	hold	own	
carry	hot	pick	
clean	hurt	seven	
cut	if	shall	
done	keep	show	
draw	kind	six	
drink	laugh	small	
eight	light	start	
fall	long	ten	
far	much	today	
full	myself	together	

Track.

about about

Write.

Color.

about about

Write the word to finish the sentence.

I learned _______ Thanksgiving.

Write your own sentence using the word <u>about</u>.

Track.

better better

Write.

Color.

better better

Write the word to finish the sentence.

Do you feel _______?

Write your own sentence using the word <u>better</u>.

Track.

Write.

Color.

Write the word to finish the sentence.

I will ________ my paper home.

Write your own sentence using the word <u>bring.</u>

Track.

Write.

Color.

Write the word to finish the sentence.

________ the groceries to the car.

Write your own sentence using the word <u>carry.</u>

Track.

clean clean clean

Write.

Color.

clean clean clean

Write the word to finish the sentence.

_______ up your mess.

Write your own sentence using the word <u>clean.</u>

Track.

cut cut cut

Write.

Color.

cut cut cut

Write the word to finish the sentence.

I _______ my finger.

Write your own sentence using the word <u>cut.</u>

Track.

done   done   done

Write.

Color.

done done done

Write the word to finish the sentence.

I am _______ with my work.

Write your own sentence using the word <u>done.</u>

Track.

draw   draw   draw

Write.

Color.

draw draw draw

Write the word to finish the sentence.

He will _______ a picture.

Write your own sentence using the word <u>draw.</u>

Track.

drink drink drink

Write.

Color.

drink drink drink

Write the word to finish the sentence.

Get a _________ from the fountain.

Write your own sentence using the word <u>drink.</u>

Track.

eight eight eight

Write.

Color.

eight eight

Write the word to finish the sentence.

She is _________ years old.

Write your own sentence using the word <u>eight.</u>

Track.

Write.

Color.

fall fall fall

Write the word to finish the sentence.

Don't _________ off the jungle gym.

Write your own sentence using the word <u>fall</u>.

Track.

Write.

Color.

far far far far

Write the word to finish the sentence.

I live _________ from here.

Write your own sentence using the word <u>far</u>.

Track.

full full full

Write.

Color.

full full full

Write the word to finish the sentence.

The basket is _______ of apples.

Write your own sentence using the word <u>full</u>.

Track.

got got got got

Write.

Color.

got got got got

Write the word to finish the sentence.

She _______ sick.

Write your own sentence using the word <u>got</u>.

Track.

grow grow grow

Write.

Color.

grow grow

Write the word to finish the sentence.

The seed will __________ into a plant.

Write your own sentence using the word <u>grow.</u>

Track.

hold hold hold

Write.

Color.

hold hold hold

Write the word to finish the sentence.

__________ onto the railing.

Write your own sentence using the word <u>hold.</u>

Track.

hot   hot   hot

Write.

Color.

hot hot hot

Write the word to finish the sentence.

She gave him a _______ drink.

Write your own sentence using the word <u>hot.</u>

Track.

hurt   hurt   hurt

Write.

Color.

hurt hurt hurt

Write the word to finish the sentence.

The cut _______ very much.

Write your own sentence using the word <u>hurt.</u>

Track.

if if if if if

Write.

Color.

if if if if if

Write the word to finish the sentence.

I will be happy __________ you play.

Write your own sentence using the word <u>if.</u>

Track.

keep keep keep

Write.

Color.

keep keep keep

Write the word to finish the sentence.

__________ up the good work!

Write your own sentence using the word <u>keep.</u>

Track.

kind   kind   kind

Write.

Color.

kind kind kind

Write the word to finish the sentence.

Be _______ to others.

Write your own sentence using the word <u>kind.</u>

Track.

laugh laugh laugh

Write.

Color.

laugh laugh

Write the word to finish the sentence.

I heard them _______ at the joke.

Write your own sentence using the word <u>laugh.</u>

Track.

light light light

Write.

Color.

light light

Write the word to finish the sentence.

Turn on the ______.

Write your own sentence using the word <u>light.</u>

Track.

long long long

Write.

Color.

long long long

Write the word to finish the sentence.

Her hair is ______ .

Write your own sentence using the word <u>long.</u>

Track.

much much much

Write.

Color.

much much much

Write the word to finish the sentence.

How _______ does that cost?

Write your own sentence using the word <u>much.</u>

Track.

myself myself

Write.

Color.

myself myself

Write the word to finish the sentence.

I hurt _______ .

Write your own sentence using the word <u>myself.</u>

Track.

never never never

Write.

Color.

never never

Write the word to finish the sentence.

I've __________ been to Disney World.

Write your own sentence using the word never.

Track.

only   only   only

Write.

Color.

only only only

Write the word to finish the sentence.

I __________ read two pages.

Write your own sentence using the word only.

Track.

own   own   own

Write.

Color.

own own own

Write the word to finish the sentence.

Use your _______ pencil.

Write your own sentence using the word OWN.

Track.

pick   pick   pick

Write.

Color.

pick pick pick

Write the word to finish the sentence.

_______ a name from the hat.

Write your own sentence using the word pick.

Track.

seven   seven

Write.

Color.

seven seven

Write the word to finish the sentence.

I am going to be _______ years old.

Write your own sentence using the word <u>seven.</u>

Track.

shall   shall   shall

Write.

Color.

shall shall shall

Write the word to finish the sentence.

What _______ I wear?

Write your own sentence using the word <u>shall.</u>

Track.

show   show   show

Write.

Color.

show show show

Write the word to finish the sentence.

I will _________ you the picture.

Write your own sentence using the word <u>show.</u>

Track.

six   six   six   six

Write.

Color.

six six six six

Write the word to finish the sentence.

There are _______ kids on the swings.

Write your own sentence using the word <u>six.</u>

Track.

small small small

Write.

Color.

small small small

Write the word to finish the sentence.

My shoes are too _______.

Write your own sentence using the word <u>small.</u>

Track.

start start

Write.

Color.

start start

Write the word to finish the sentence.

School will _______ soon.

Write your own sentence using the word <u>start.</u>

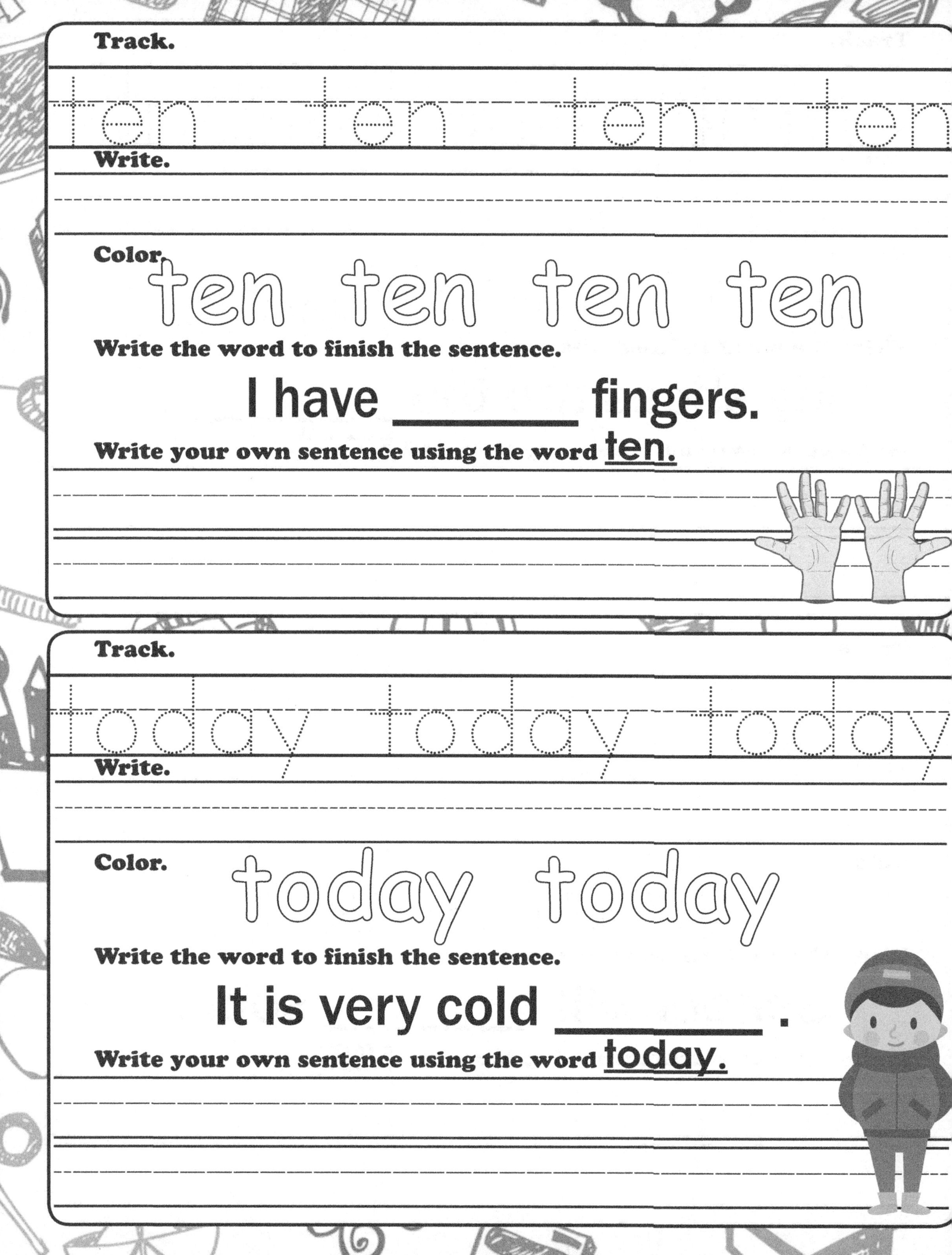

Track.

ten ten ten ten

Write.

Color.

ten ten ten ten

Write the word to finish the sentence.

I have _______ fingers.

Write your own sentence using the word <u>ten.</u>

Track.

today today today

Write.

Color.

today today

Write the word to finish the sentence.

It is very cold _______ .

Write your own sentence using the word <u>today.</u>

Track.

together together

Write.

Color.

together together

Write the word to finish the sentence.

Let's play __________ .

Write your own sentence using the word <u>together.</u>

Track.

try try try

Write.

Color.

try try try

Write the word to finish the sentence.

Please __________ to be quiet.

Write your own sentence using the word <u>try.</u>

Track.

warm warm warm

Write.

Color.

warm warm warm

Write the word to finish the sentence.

The soup is _______ .

Write your own sentence using the word <u>warm.</u>

Made in the USA
Monee, IL
07 July 2026

56551533R00070